THE HEART
OF WORSHIP
DEVOTIONAL

Devotions Inspired by the Song

HONOR **HB** BOOKS

Inspiration and Motivation for the Seasons of Life

COOK COMMUNICATIONS MINISTRIES
Colorado Springs, Colorado • Paris, Ontario
KINGSWAY COMMUNICATIONS LTD
Eastbourne, England

Honor® is an imprint of
Cook Communications Ministries, Colorado Springs, CO 80918
Cook Communications, Paris, Ontario
Kingsway Communications, Eastbourne, England

THE HEART OF WORSHIP
© 2006 by Honor Books

Devotions by Adam Palmer.

Cover Design: BMB Design
Interior Photo: © Brand X Pictures / PictureQuest

First Printing, 2006
Printed in United States of America

1 2 3 4 5 6 7 8 9 10 Printing/Year 10 09 08 07 06

Library of Congress Cataloging-in-Publication Data

Heart of worship : devotions inspired by the song.
     p. cm. -- (30 days of worship)
  ISBN 1-56292-732-9
 1. Christian life--Meditations. I. Honor Books. II. Series.
 BV4501.3.H43 2006
 242--dc22
                                    2005030419

Introduction

In our world of glitz and glamour, flash and fantasy, it's so easy to forget what worship is really about. Worship isn't about well-rehearsed musicians, top-notch sound systems, emotional cheerleading, or clever wordplay.

It should be all about Jesus.

Matt Redman wrote the song "The Heart of Worship" as a prayer of contrition and forgiveness. The song stands as a stark reminder to the church of what—and whom—our worship should focus upon.

The aim of this book is to help you take a closer look at the true motivations behind worship over the next month. May you be blessed by the words you find here. May you read them with a heart of contrition instead of condemnation.

May you truly discover your heart of worship.

The Heart of Worship

BY MATT REDMAN

When the music fades
And all is stripped away and I simply come
Longing just to bring something that's of worth
That will bless your heart

I'll bring you more than a song, for a song in
itself
Is not what you have required. You search much
deeper within
Through the way things appear. You're looking
into my heart

I'm coming back to the heart of worship
And it's all about you, all about you, Jesus
I'm sorry, Lord, for the thing I've made it
When it's all about you, all about you, Jesus

King of endless worth, no one could express
How much you deserve.
Though I'm weak and poor
All I have is yours, every single breath

DAY 1: When the Music Fades

Now the Spirit of the LORD had departed from Saul, and an evil spirit from the LORD tormented him. Saul's attendants said to him, "See, an evil spirit from God is tormenting you. Let our lord command his servants here to search for someone who can play the harp. He will play when the evil spirit from God comes upon you, and you will feel better." So Saul said to his attendants, "Find someone who plays well and bring him to me." ... David came to Saul and entered his service. Saul liked him very much, and David became one of his armor-bearers. Then Saul sent word to Jesse, saying, "Allow David to remain in my service, for I am pleased with him." Whenever the spirit from God came upon Saul, David would take his harp and play. Then relief would come to Saul; he would feel better, and the evil spirit would leave him.

—1 SAMUEL 16:14–17, 21–23

*But an evil spirit from the L*ORD *came upon Saul as he was sitting in his house with his spear in his hand. While David was playing the harp, Saul tried to pin him to the wall with his spear, but David eluded him as Saul drove the spear into the wall. That night David made good his escape.*

—1 SAMUEL 19:9–10

The heart of worship is more than music.

Has a song ever helped you through some trial in your life? We've all had times when we were going through some hardship and we've listened to a certain song and found a small amount of relief from our distress.

But when the song ends, has our hardship disappeared? Do a few chords miraculously set everything right in life? Of course not. When the music ends, we are still faced with whatever challenges we had before the song began.

In the case of Saul, music—specifically, music played by David—soothed him and eased his torment. But it wasn't gone after one application of David's harp playing. The evil spirit that tormented Saul returned again and again. Each time David's playing only eased and soothed Saul but did not solve the king's problems.

No matter how much music Saul heard his problems didn't go away, because Saul's problem wasn't with his ears—it was with his heart. Instead of repenting from the evil ways that had caused this spirit to come upon him, he treated the symptoms and sought only quick relief.

Saul forgot God is the real issue and instead focused on the music. For him, it became all about the music. But music isn't forever.

In our worship, we must make sure we are focused on the right thing—our eternal God and Savior. Why? Because worship isn't about music—music is only a secondary part of worship.

The heart of worship is a heart that is focused simply on God himself.

Prayer for the Day:

God, I'm thankful for the music you created. I'm glad you've given me the ability to worship you through music. But, Lord, I pray that you'll help me to remember the true heart of worship—you. I choose today to focus on you, to align my heart in your direction. And in so doing, I pray that you would accept my act of worship. Amen.

DAY 2:
And All Is
Stripped
Away

Since we have these promises, dear friends, let us purify ourselves from everything that contaminates body and spirit,
perfecting holiness out of reverence for God.

—2 CORINTHIANS 7:1

The heart of worship is purification.

Water purifiers are amazing things. The water from your tap could be the worst-tasting water on the block, but run it through a purifier and it becomes miraculously transformed into a great-tasting water that's worth bottling.

Purification.

It strains out harmful or offensive chemicals and minerals in the water and leaves only the water in its purest form. Purified water is simply water, with nothing extra or artificial.

Purification.

Today's Scripture passage follows directly after a passage that speaks of God living among his people and walking with us. We are encouraged to strip away uncleanness and idolatry in order to purify our hearts—and we're encouraged to do it out of reverence for God. That is the heart of worship.

Purification for the sake of purification. Stripping away everything that isn't God in order to honor everything that is. We are called to be purified so that we might flow freely and clearly toward God—and others—free of contaminants and easily accessible.

The thing with water purifiers is that they must be in constant use. We can't put a filter on our tap one day and expect the water to continue to be purified if we take it off or let the filter get contaminated. That water needs constant purification.

The heart of worship is a heart that continually strives to be purified as it continually pours itself out.

Prayer for the Day:

O God, you're so wonderful. Purify my heart, Lord. This is a two-person process, God, so I pray that you'll help me do my part and help me get out of your way as you do your part. I want to have a pure heart in all I do. I want to worship you with pure motives. Thank you, Lord. Amen.

DAY 3: And I Simply Come

When the people saw the thunder and lightning and heard the trumpet and saw the mountain in smoke, they trembled with fear. They stayed at a distance and said to Moses, "Speak to us yourself and we will listen. But do not have God speak to us or we will die." Moses said to the people, "Do not be afraid. God has come to test you, so that the fear of God will be with you to keep you from sinning." The people remained at a distance, while Moses approached the thick darkness where God was.

—Exodus 20:18–21

The heart of worship is approach.

"Do not be afraid." Over and over in Scripture, we hear this phrase when people are face-to-face with God. Again and again, he tells them not to be afraid to approach him. He created us to be creatures in relationship with him. Just look at the garden of Eden, where God walked with Adam on a daily basis.

God wants us to be unafraid to approach him. He yearns for interaction with his greatest creation; he longs to spend quality time with the ones he loves. He invites us to come to him, just as we are. The Israelites were scared of God, but Moses encouraged them to approach God, even though they were sinful people. They didn't have to be rid of their sin before they came—they simply had to have hearts that were motivated to be pure.

God wants us to have a heart of approach. He wants us to come to him in simplicity and full of reverence. It doesn't have to be a big show, and we don't need to come with a stockpile of five-dollar words to impress God.

We just have to come.

Don't be afraid. Just come. For that is the heart of worship.

Prayer for the Day:

God, thank you for opening up a way of approach. Thank you for loving me despite my flaws and failures. Thank you for working in me to eliminate those flaws and failures. Lord, I want to commune with you the same way Adam did at the beginning of time. I want to come to you simply, so that I might know you better and better. I love you so much, Lord. Amen.

DAY 4:
Longing
Just to
Bring
Something
That's of
Worth

When Boaz had finished eating and drinking and was in good spirits, he went over to lie down at the far end of the grain pile. Ruth approached quietly, uncovered his feet and lay down. In the middle of the night something startled the man, and he turned and discovered a woman lying at his feet. "Who are you?" he asked. "I am your servant Ruth," she said. "Spread the corner of your garment over me, since you are a kinsman-redeemer." "The Lord bless you, my daughter," he replied. "This kindness is greater than that which you showed earlier: You have not run after the younger men, whether rich or poor. And now, my daughter, don't be afraid. I will do for you all you ask. All my fellow townsmen know that you are a woman of noble character."

—Ruth 3:7–11

The heart of worship is eagerness.

Ruth had nothing. A foreigner in a foreign land (she was originally from Moab but was now living in Israel), Ruth had recently lost her husband, and she now lived with her widowed mother-in-law, Naomi. Being a woman of noble character, Ruth had taken it upon herself to take care of Naomi, so she'd begun gleaning the fields of Boaz, a great man in the nation and also a relative of hers through Naomi. Boaz was exceedingly kind to Ruth and began to provide for her above and beyond what she needed.

Upon hearing this news, Naomi encouraged Ruth to approach Boaz in the night and offer herself to him in marriage. Under the laws of that day, male relatives had a responsibility to marry widows, and since Boaz was a relative who'd shown kindness to Ruth, Naomi thought he would accept her offer, which he did.

What does this have to do with worship? Ruth had nothing to give, really, except herself.

Ruth's offer of marriage didn't bring anything to Boaz except the obligation to accept it. She was potentially setting herself up for a loveless marriage full of rejection. Yet she was eager to do it. Why?

Because she knew Boaz's character. He'd shown himself to be a kind, caring man who favored her, so Ruth knew there was little risk in marrying him. Boaz, in turn, saw Ruth's offer as a generous and gracious one, and he immediately praised her kindness to him.

We know God's character. We know that God will accept our humble offerings with kindness. It is his nature.

We know we don't really have anything to bring to him that he doesn't already have, yet we present ourselves eagerly.

Prayer for the Day:

Heavenly Father, I don't have much to give
you. I look around at the magnificent world
you've created, and I feel small—a little like a
widow gleaning your harvest fields.
Nevertheless, I know that you look upon me
with favor; I know that you've exalted me,
and I thank you for it. I'm eager to do what-
ever you ask of me, Lord. It is my heart's
desire. I'm listening. Amen.

DAY 5:
That Will Bless Your Heart

I scrub my hands with purest soap, then join hands with the others in the great circle, dancing around your altar, GOD, singing God-songs at the top of my lungs, telling God-stories.... I'm on the level with you, GOD; I bless you every chance I get.

—PSALM 26:6–7, 12 MSG

The heart of worship is dedication.

What does it mean to bless God's heart? What does that term imply for us as worshippers today? How can we come close to knowing what will indeed bless God?

In addition to being known as Israel's greatest king, David is also considered one of history's greatest worshippers. When it came to worshipping God, David pretty much had a corner on the market. And in this psalm, he gives a hint as to what will bless God.

David praised with abandon. He joined in with others, singing at the top of his lungs. He was dedicated to his worship.

So let's make sure we have this straight—here is a well-known king of Israel worshipping in front of other people and singing to God like crazy. He isn't worried about his kingly image; he isn't concerned with politics or rebellions or taxes or anything else kings concerned themselves with. Instead, he's laying all that aside and dedicating himself to God in that moment of worship. In his worship, he wasn't King David—he was just God's loyal servant, seeking to bless God's heart.

Strive to dedicate your heart to God as you worship.

Prayer for the Day:

Dear God, I dedicate myself to you. Thank you for accepting me. Thank you for listening to me. Thank you for hearing me when I cry out in worship to you. I know I can't stay dedicated to you on my own—there are too many distractions, too many rabbit trails to wander down. Please help me to look to you continually. Please help me to worship you with dedication and abandon, so that I might bless your heart. Amen.

DAY 6: I'll Bring You More Than a Song

No man should appear before the LORD empty-handed: Each of you must bring a gift in proportion to the way the LORD your God has blessed you.

—DEUTERONOMY 16:16–17

The heart of worship is giving back to God.

Finally, the harvest was over. The farmers of Israel had planted earlier in the year, they'd tended their crops, watched them grow, and the time to bring in the crop had come. They'd worked hard, and now the harvest was in—their labors had paid off. It was time to celebrate.

This passage in Deuteronomy comes from the law of Moses, and it concerns a certain feast known as the "Feast of Tabernacles." This feasting time was a time of joy that came immediately after the harvest had been brought in, and it served as a way for the Israelites to acknowledge God's hand on their farming efforts.

But one of the critical portions of this particular feast was the gift. This was one of three annual feasts in which every man in Israel was obligated to appear before the Lord in worship, and during each of those times, every man had to bring something to God. It didn't matter what it was, so long as it was "in proportion to" God's blessing on them.

God didn't want cheap worship. He wanted the Israelites to recognize all that he had given them that year, and he wanted them to give back some of it as a means of focusing their hearts back toward him in thanks for their bountiful crop.

God doesn't want cheap worship from us, either. He wants us to give back to him, to give of ourselves as we worship.

God wants us to be willing to do whatever he asks of us and, in so doing, to give to him a portion of what he's so graciously given to us.

Prayer for the Day:

God, thanks for all that you've given me. Sometimes I have to look hard to see it, but I recognize the times you've blessed me finan- cially, relationally, spiritually, emotionally, and physically. And I'll admit it—sometimes it's hard for me to give back. But I remember that it's all yours anyway, Lord, so I pray that you'll give me the strength to give back to you with a sincere and grateful heart, however you want me to. I want to give you so much more than just a song, God. I want to give you my heart. Amen.

DAY 7: I'll Bring You More Than a Song

Everyone who was willing and whose heart moved him came and brought an offering to the LORD for the work on the Tent of Meeting, for all its service, and for the sacred garments. All who were willing, men and women alike, came and brought gold jewelry of all kinds: brooches, earrings, rings and ornaments. They all presented their gold as a wave offering to the LORD. Everyone who had blue, purple or scarlet yarn or fine linen, or goat hair, ram skins dyed red or hides of sea cows brought them. Those presenting an offering of silver or bronze brought it as an offering to *the L<small>ORD</small>, and everyone who had acacia wood for any part of the work brought it. Every skilled woman spun with her hands and brought what she had spun—blue, purple or scarlet yarn or fine linen. And all the women who were willing and had the skill spun the goat hair. The leaders brought onyx stones and other gems to be mounted on the ephod and breastpiece. They also brought spices and olive oil for the light and for the anointing oil and for the fragrant incense. All the Israelite men and women who were willing brought to the L<small>ORD</small> freewill offerings for all the work the L<small>ORD</small> through Moses had commanded them to do.*

—E<small>XODUS</small> 35:21–29

The heart of worship is giving what you have.

Potluck suppers are a ubiquitous part of the American church experience. They're not always called "potluck suppers," as the term ranges based on denominations and geographical regions, but as a rule we've all experienced this type of meal at least once, if not several times. Everyone brings something different, and together there is a big dinner for all to share.

Now, imagine that instead of having a potluck supper, the Israelites were having a potluck tent construction. God had given them instructions on building the Tent of Meeting, the portable tabernacle where he would reside until they reached the Promised Land and were able to build him something a little more permanent. He was very specific about the materials to be used, and everyone in Israel consulted the list and brought what he or she had.

No one was required to bring one of everything. No one was required to provide all of one material. The only requirement was that people gave what they already had, and in so doing, the job got done.

God has given each of us different talents, abilities, and blessings. Things that he'd like us to give back to him.

Give what you have and watch God orchestrate it to bless others. This is the heart of worship.

Prayer for the Day:

Thanks, God. Thank you for what you've given me. Please forgive me for the times I've been jealous of other people's talents and dissatisfied with my own. I realize that's not part of your plan. Help me to give what I have, Lord. I'm grateful for what I've received, and I pray for your guidance in giving it back to you. Amen.

DAY 8:
A Song in Itself Is Not What You Have Required

Hezekiah assigned the priests and Levites to divisions—each of them according to their duties as priests or Levites—to offer burnt offerings and fellowship offerings, to minister, to give thanks and to sing praises at the gates of the LORD's dwelling.

—2 CHRONICLES 31:2

The heart of worship is diverse.

In an effort to create health awareness in this country, lawmakers have recently enacted a law that makes bicycling the only legal form of transportation. You are no longer permitted to drive an automobile. Motorcycles aren't allowed either. Boats? Only if they're paddleboats. The air travel industry is reeling from the implications of the new law, as is the railway industry. Also, walking is strictly prohibited and is punishable by imprisonment and a hefty fine.

Of course, this is a fantastical illustration. This crazy law doesn't exist—or does it? As a whole, we've gotten so wrapped up in using music as a form of communal worship that we forget there are other ways of worshipping. In fact, the term "praise and worship" is often code for "fast songs and slow songs."

But there's so much more to worship than just singing. Today's passage mentions the Levites—a tribe in Israel that was devoted to the priesthood. The priests were men who lived and breathed worship, and you'll notice that singing was the *last* priority in their list of duties. Offerings (both to atone for sin and just to be relational with God), ministering, thanksgiving … these things are also forms of worship.

Worship isn't about how eloquently or passionately you sing a song. It isn't about great guitar tone or clever lyrical wordplay or finding the perfect harmony notes.

Worship is about our hearts responding to God—in whatever way we see fit according to our personality.

We can worship God in the everyday duties of our lives. It's the heart that matters, not the action.

Prayer for the Day:

God, I thank you for the ability you've given me to worship. I thank you for the many ways I can respond to you, that I can use whatever you've given me as a means of worship. I love you, Lord, and I pray that you'll accept my worship when I offer it with the right heart. Amen.

DAY 9: A Song in Itself Is Not What You Have Required

Ascribe to the LORD, O families of nations, ascribe to the LORD glory and strength, ascribe to the LORD the glory due his name. Bring an offering and come before him; worship the LORD in the splendor of his holiness. Tremble before him, all the earth! The world is firmly established; it cannot be moved. Let the heavens rejoice, let the earth be glad; let them say among the nations, "The LORD reigns!"

—1 CHRONICLES 16:28–31

The heart of worship is awed by God.

Take a look around you right now. Better yet, put this book down, head outside (if you can), and take a look around you. What do you see? Is the sun out, or is it overcast? Are the trees in full bloom, or are they leafless (or somewhere in between)? Do you see any flowers? Bushes? Shrubs? What sorts of creatures do you see, if any? Are the stars out? Can you make out any constellations? What phase is the moon in? Can you find Mars, Venus, or Mercury without a telescope?

Okay, come back in and resume reading. Think about what you've just seen. Get a panoramic picture in your mind of all that your eyes just took in.

God made it. All of it.

Even the buildings you might have seen were, in a sense, made by God, as he placed the raw materials on this earth to create the stuff those buildings were made from. God made *everything* you just saw.

God is so much greater than any of our words or songs could ever express. If we can begin to look at God with the awe that's due his name, all our other actions toward him will fall into line. This is indeed the heart of worship.

Prayer for the Day:

Lord God, I look around and I can't even believe what I see. I stand in awe at what you've done, the great things you've created. You're amazing, God, and I thank you for creating this wonderful world for me to exist in. I praise you and worship you, Lord, and I pray that you'll help me to appreciate all you've made and give you glory for it. Amen.

DAY 10: You Search Much Deeper Within

The LORD does not look at the things man looks at. Man looks at the outward appearance, but the LORD looks at the heart.

—1 SAMUEL 16:7

The heart of worship is introspective.

Imagine for a moment that you're a deep-sea explorer. You're the best in the business, and you've been searching for years to find the location of a wrecked Spanish galleon that, legend has it, was packed with gold when it went down. The ocean depths have hidden the secret for centuries, and now, after your own years of exploration, you've finally discovered the sunken vessel.

So you pack your gear and head down into the depths to see what you can find. Deeper and deeper you descend until you come upon the ship and begin searching it—carefully, gingerly, to avoid kicking up unnecessary dust. You're down there for a while when suddenly you catch a glint of metal through the dim, flickering light coming through the water. You've just found the treasure!

What do you do with it? Do you leave it there, content that you've found it? Of course not—

you begin to make preparations to salvage and restore the treasure. The search was for naught unless you act on what you've found.

In the same way, God searches the inmost depths of our hearts, but his searching does us no good unless we turn ourselves inward and search along with him and act on what he reveals to us. God will show us things he wants us to see, but we in turn must make preparations to do something about what we're shown. If he shows us something good, we must pull up the treasure and use it. If he shows us something we need to change, we must have the courage to do so.

God searches our innermost depths; let us not be afraid to voyage with him.

Prayer for the Day:

Dear Lord, I thank you for what you've done in my heart. I thank you for searching deeply so that I might serve you better. Give me the courage to act on what you show me. Give me grace where I need it, and give me wisdom so that I might serve you well. Amen.

DAY 11: You Search Much Deeper Within

And you, my son Solomon, acknowledge the God of your father, and serve him with wholehearted devotion and with a willing mind, for the LORD searches every heart and understands every motive behind the thoughts. If you seek him, he will be found by you; but if you forsake him, he will reject you forever. Consider now, for the LORD has chosen you to build a temple as a sanctuary. Be strong and do the work.

—1 CHRONICLES 28:9–10

The heart of worship is willing.

King David had it in his heart to build a permanent temple where God could dwell, but he just couldn't make it happen in his lifetime. On his deathbed, he gave a long speech to his son Solomon, who was about to take over the kingship of Israel. Today's passage comes from that speech, where David is exhorting Solomon to take up his mantle and build the temple David always wanted to build.

So, just what is one of the main requirements for constructing the ultimate house of worship made by man? Solomon had to serve God with a willing heart and mind. If Solomon hadn't done that, the temple would never have been built. Instead, he would have been rejected as king, and only the Lord knows what would have happened.

It is the same with us. If we sincerely want to build a heart of worship, we must have willing hearts and minds to do it. God is searching our hearts, looking for our motives—especially when we worship. We must create willingness to follow him, to "be strong and do the work" that he has called us to do. In Solomon's case, that work was building the temple, a task he eventually accomplished with gusto.

What is the work you're called to do? Whatever it is, when you do it with willingness, you are doing it with a heart of worship.

Prayer for the Day:

O God, I'm willing. I'm willing to do whatever you ask of me. Thank you for including me in your plans, and thank you for giving me the chance to worship you. My heart and mind are willing to follow you anywhere, even the places that may frighten me. I love you, God. Amen.

DAY 12: Through the Way Things Appear

In the same way, the Spirit helps us in our weakness. We do not know what we ought to pray for, but the Spirit himself intercedes for us with groans that words cannot express. And he who searches our hearts knows the mind of the Spirit, because the Spirit intercedes for the saints in accordance with God's will.

—ROMANS 8:26–27

The heart of worship is trusting.

Six-year-old Laurel is having trouble going to sleep. She's afraid of the dark, and though she has an aquarium in her room that casts a fair amount of light in her direction, it still isn't enough. She hears cars rumbling down the road outside and the bubbling of the aquarium's filter. Her closet door is open, and the light allows her to see only a yawning chasm of blackness inside it. Her toys are casting odd shadows on the floor. The longer she lies in the dark, the more her imagination runs wild and the more scared she becomes.

Meanwhile, her parents lie in the room adjacent to her, oblivious to her fear. Why? Because they see the bigger picture. They know that her fright, however real to her, is irrational. They know there's nothing in her closet to be afraid of. They know that the cars are just passing by and that the aquarium is just doing its job. They know that the toys pose no danger (except to bare feet).

Laurel calls out to her parents to come ease her fears, and they go in for the third time that night and pray with her. They do their best to help her realize what's really going on and kiss her goodnight. Eventually, she trusts them and falls asleep.

Appearances can frequently be deceiving, and with God things often aren't as they seem. God sees the big picture; he has a master plan. So when we begin to get frightened at the surroundings of our lives, we must remember young Laurel and how much easier her night would have gone if she'd just trusted her parents in the first place and gone to sleep in peace. She was safe. So are we.

The heart of worship approaches God with trust.

Prayer for the Day:

God, I know that you see everything much more clearly than I do. Thanks for looking after me like a father for his child. Help me to trust you with everything, God, and forgive me for the times I don't. I love you. Amen.

DAY 13: You're Looking into My Heart

Search me, O God, and know my heart; test me and know my anxious thoughts. See if there is any offensive way in me, and lead me in the way everlasting.

—PSALM 139:23–24

Prayer for the Day:

God, thanks for your correction. It sounds weird to say that, but it's true. Without your correction, I'd be lost and out of the game. So thanks for pointing me in the right direction. Lord, it's hard to see where I'm headed down here, but I trust your guidance, and I rely on your correction. You're so mighty. Amen.

DAY 14: You're Looking into My Heart

The lamp of the LORD searches the spirit of a man; it searches out his inmost being.

—PROVERBS 20:27

The heart of worship is open.

At this very moment, we are all being bombarded by electromagnetic waves. Whether we like it or not, they are all around us, carrying information invisibly through the air. Radio waves, X-ray waves, light waves are there, actively doing what they do.

Radio waves, for example, are specific frequencies of the electromagnetic spectrum. Grab an FM receiver with an antenna, and you can tune in the slightest of those frequencies to hear what the sender wants you to hear. Turn the dial, and you'll hear something different. The sender (radio station) doesn't wait to broadcast until you turn on your radio; he's broadcasting all the time, whether you're listening or not. It's up to you to listen.

God is actively looking inside our hearts, searching out our innermost being. He is penetrating our souls like radio waves penetrate the air. But are we tuned in to him? Are we listening to the messages he's sending?

The great thing about radio waves is that you don't have to have the best radio in the world to listen—any inexpensive receiver will do. In the same way, we don't have to have flawless hearts in order to hear from God … we just have to have open ones.

We must be willing to tune in to his broadcast and listen to whatever he has to say.

Prayer for the Day:

Heavenly Father, thank you for loving me so much that you speak into my life. Thank you for searching out the innermost parts of my heart and being. Help me to listen to your frequency, God. Teach me to keep my dial tuned in to you. You're amazing, God, and I love you. Amen.

DAY 15: I'm Coming Back to the Heart of Worship

Therefore, brothers, since we have confidence to enter the Most Holy Place by the blood of Jesus, by a new and living way opened for us through the curtain, that is, his body, and since we have a great priest over the house of God, let us draw near to God with a sincere heart in full assurance of faith, having our hearts sprinkled to cleanse us from a guilty conscience and having our bodies washed with pure water.

—HEBREWS 10:19–22

The heart of worship is receptive.

It's easy to take for granted the massive, multi-layered work that Jesus did on the cross. Before he died, worshipping God was a very formal affair. To do it properly, one had to travel to Jerusalem and worship at the temple there, for that is where God dwelled. It involved animals and bloodletting, fire and priests. It involved special articles of worship, constructed to God's exact specifications.

And then came Jesus, who made the ultimate sacrifice. He offered his blood, and all those Old Testament requirements for worship were knocked on their collective ears. No longer was a priest required. Nor an animal or grain sacrifice. Nor even a physical temple.

Jesus made a way for us to approach God directly, "in full assurance of faith." He did an amazing thing on the cross, and so often we think of how that work purchased our salvation, forgetting that it did other things as well.

And so part of the heart of worship becomes receiving all that Jesus did. All that he offers. The heart of worship is receptive to his many works.

Let us approach God in full assurance, knowing that he receives us by the blood of Christ.

Prayer for the Day:

Jesus, I'm amazed at your love for me. Thank you so much for the sacrifice you made on the cross. Thank you for providing a way for me to worship you. I'm so glad you did. And I do worship you. I pray that you'll instill in me a heart of worship that always seeks after you and that remembers what you've done for me. I can't begin to thank you enough. Amen.

DAY 16:
I'm Coming
Back to the
Heart of
Worship

One of the teachers of the law came and heard them debating. Noticing that Jesus had given them a good answer, he asked him, "Of all the commandments, which is the most important?" "The most important one," answered Jesus, "is this: 'Hear, O Israel, the Lord our God, the Lord is one. Love the Lord your God with all your heart and with all your soul and with all your mind and with all your strength.' The second is this: 'Love your neighbor as yourself.' There is no commandment greater than these." "Well said, teacher," the man replied. "You are right in saying that God is one and there is no other but him. To love him with all your heart, with all your understanding and with all your strength, and to love your neighbor as yourself is more important than all burnt offerings and sacrifices." When Jesus saw that he had answered wisely, he said to him, "You are not far from the kingdom of God."

—MARK 12:28–34

The heart of worship is love.

Today's Scripture passage tells a great story of Jesus' interaction with some of the intellectual greats of his day. Jesus was discussing the law of Moses with many different teachers of that law. As a rabbi, Jesus was no slouch in his knowledge of the law either. These guys had dedicated their lives to studying the Mosaic law, and they were astounded by how much Jesus knew of it.

The Mosaic law consisted of many commandments, most of which had to do with specific actions and codes of conduct. Pick any random verse in Leviticus or Deuteronomy, and you'll most likely find details on offerings and sacrifices, regulations on cleanliness, punishments for specific transgressions—basically a whole lot of rules. Those books aren't entirely rules, but they often feel that way when you're reading them.

And then Jesus gets put on the spot about the law and immediately quotes from those two books. The first commandment he lists is from Deuteronomy 6:4–5. The second is Leviticus 19:18. Jesus saw through all the rules and distilled them to their essence: love. Love God and love others. It all boils down to love.

Love.

It's more important than burnt offerings and sacrifices.

Love is the most important thing we can do in our lives, including in our worship. Love is a commandment that has spanned the ages, applying to both the Old and New Testaments.

Love is the basis of the heart of worship.

Prayer for the Day:

God, I love you. I really, really love you. I know I don't always act like it, but I do. And I know that I only love you because you loved me first, so I thank you for loving me. God, I'm pretty good with that first commandment, but I need help with the second one. Help me to love others and, in so doing, worship you.

Amen.

DAY 17: And It's All about You

Not to us, O LORD, not to us but to your name be the glory, because of your love and faithfulness.

—PSALM 115:1

The heart of worship is not about itself.

Think of how your Sunday morning worship service has changed over the past twenty years. Most likely the lights are dimmer, and the music is louder and more contemporary. Computers are used to project the lyrics (and complementing images, sometimes). The songs themselves have taken on a more Top 40 radio format, with a verse/chorus/verse/chorus/bridge/chorus/chorus layout, instead of the standard four-refrain hymn motif.

All these changes have served the music well, but they've also done something else ... they've obscured the heart of worship. Looking back at the Bible, we can see that when people praised God with music, they used culturally relevant instrumentation, so it isn't wrong to incorporate technological advances and cultural changes into our worship. But we cannot focus simply on those changes.

There's a temptation to soak ourselves in the outward appearances of worship. To clap because the music's loud and the beat lends itself to clapping. To raise our hands because we hear the emotional cues in the leader's voice and in the musical arrangement.

But it's supposed to be all about God.

All of it.

We are there to worship, not to experience a concert or light show.

The true heart of worship gives glory only to God, not to itself. It is indeed all about him.

Prayer for the Day:

Holy Father God, thank you for progress. I thank you that I get to live in a time of such marvelous innovation. But thank you most of all for hearing my worship—no matter what it looks or sounds like. You're awesome, God, and I want to make my worship only about you. Amen.

DAY 18: All about You, Jesus

The Lord says: "These people come near to me with their mouth and honor me with their lips, but their hearts are far from me. Their worship of me is made up only of rules taught by men."

—ISAIAH 29:13

The heart of worship is honest through and through.

Mary used to answer the phone for a living. She was the receptionist for a small business that employed about fifty people, but her bosses wanted it to sound like a big, thriving corporation, so they gave her a specific line to answer the phone: "It's a great day at [Company Name]! How may I direct your call?" They wanted her to say it with enthusiasm, so the people on the other end of the line could hear her smiling.

She dove in with gusto, and the first few times, she gave it all she had. "It's a *great* day at [Company Name]! *How* may I direct your call?!" But as the days wore on, her cheeks began to get sore from the smiling, and her voice just couldn't handle the emotion. Her enthusiasm for the phrase began to wane. She still said it the same way, but it began to lose its emotion. After her first few weeks on the job, the phrase had merely become a mechanical way of answering the phone. Outwardly, it had all the inflection the bosses wanted it to have, but Mary's heart was no longer in it.

In today's passage, God spoke these words about the city of Jerusalem, a city King David—one of Israel's greatest worshippers—had established. Like Mary, the people of Jerusalem had lost the heart of worship. They were still saying all the right things and looking good on the outside, but they weren't fooling God. He knew they were only following the rules.

The question we must answer is this: Are we going to be like this emotionally dead Jerusalem or the living Jerusalem of King David's time?

Are our hearts honest about our worship, or are we just going through the motions?

Prayer for the Day:

Lord Jesus, I worship you. My worship is all about you, Jesus. From the depths of my heart, I worship you. Jesus, I know you don't care about outward emotions—you care about what's in my heart. I pray that my heart would be full of true worship to you, because I love you. Amen.

DAY 19:
I'm Sorry, Lord, for the Thing I've Made It

"Do not be afraid," Samuel replied. "You have done all this evil; yet do not turn away from the LORD, but serve the LORD with all your heart. Do not turn away after useless idols. They can do you no good, nor can they rescue you, because they are useless. For the sake of his great name the LORD will not reject his people, because the LORD was pleased to make you his own. As for me, far be it from me that I should sin against the LORD by failing to *pray for you. And I will teach you the way that is good and right. But be sure to fear the LORD and serve him faithfully with all your heart; consider what great things he has done for you."*

—1 SAMUEL 12:20–24

The heart of worship is contrite.

God originally set up the nation of Israel as a theocracy. He was to rule over it through the judges, speaking to them and letting them deliver his word to the rest of the people.

But the neighboring countries weren't set up like this, and Israel grew restless with its arrangement. Everyone else had a king, and they wanted one, too. God told them not to ask for a king, but they asked for one anyway. It was a disobedient request, but God granted it, ending the leadership role of the judges.

In this passage, Samuel, the last ruling judge of Israel, is addressing the nation as its leader for the last time. It is amazing that, despite their rebellion in asking for a king, Samuel still implores them to follow after God. They still had the opportunity to turn to God in contrition and know that he would forgive them in an instant.

When we have a spirit of true contrition in our hearts, God readily welcomes us with open arms, no matter what mistakes we make of our lives or in our relationship with him.

If we turn to him with a contrite heart and in full repentance, he turns to us with acceptance and love.

Prayer for the Day:

Lord, thanks for hearing me when I repent. I'm sorry, Lord, for the ways I've messed up my attitudes about worship. I'm sorry for the times I've made it about something other than you. But in the midst of my contrition, I'm also glad you let me know that you accept me. Thank you, Lord, for hearing me. Amen.

DAY 20: I'm Sorry, Lord, for the Thing I've Made It

When a prayer or plea is made by any of your people Israel—each one aware of the afflictions of his own heart, and spreading out his hands toward this temple—then hear from heaven, your dwelling place. Forgive and act; deal with each man according to all he does, since you know his heart (for you alone know the hearts of all men).

—1 Kings 8:38–39

The heart of worship is repentant.

Noah was in time-out. Even though he was only three years old, he'd gotten into an argument with his five-year-old sister about a ball, and he'd pushed her down and grabbed it out of her hands. And now he was in trouble. Once his time-out was up, his mother gave him a reprimand, brought him before his sister, and made him say that magical phrase: "I'm sorry."

Two minutes later, he was back in time-out for the same offense.

Now, this is pretty typical behavior for a child. But sometimes we adults aren't any better. We can be good at feeling sorry for our actions. But how good are we at repentance? It's one thing to feel sorry; it's something altogether different to change our behavior based on those feelings.

But notice in Solomon's prayer, that he asks God to forgive *and act*. When we truly turn from our sinful, selfish attitudes, God doesn't just forgive—he acts on our behalf. Our actions of repentance lead to action from God.

When we repent—even as an act of worship to God—God then acts on our behalf, receiving the repentant worship we give him.

Prayer for the Day:

God, I thank you. Thanks for receiving my repentance. I really am sorry for the ways I've let you down and disobeyed your commands. I know I can't do this on my own, Lord. I want to change, but I need your help. Enable me to act in a way that brings glory to your name. Amen.

DAY 21: When It's All about You

You shall not make for yourself an idol in the form of anything in heaven above or on the earth beneath or in the waters below. You shall not bow down to them or worship them; for I, the LORD your God, am a jealous God, punishing the children for the sin of the fathers to the third and fourth generation of those who hate me, but showing love to a thousand generations of those who love me and keep my commandments.

—EXODUS 20:4–6

The heart of worship is monogamous toward God.

Here's a tough question: What are some modern-day idols? Sure, we know about the Baals and Ashtoreths and Asherahs of the Old Testament, but what would be an idol of our current times?

The answers are obvious at first: entertainers, musicians, movie stars, athletes, just about any celebrity. But what about hobbies? Pets? Family members?

Idolatry isn't about bowing down to a carved image anymore—it's about dividing your heart's loyalties. The true heart of worship is *all* about Jesus, drawing the line when anything threatens to overtake it.

It isn't wrong to be a fan of a certain sports team or to dote on our dogs, but when things like these begin to encroach on the importance we place on Jesus, when we begin to shirk him in order to follow these types of pursuits, we've given way to idolatry. We've shared our hearts with another.

Worship is to be all about Jesus. Let us ensure in our hearts that it is.

Prayer for the Day:

Jesus, please forgive me for cheating on you with my heart. The places of my heart where I haven't served you fully and have allowed idols in my life—I'm sorry for that. Please change me there. Remind me, Jesus, that worship is all about you, and help me to serve you with everything I have. Amen.

DAY 22: All about You, Jesus

Again, the devil took him to a very high mountain and showed him all the kingdoms of the world and their splendor. "All this I will give you," he said, "if you will bow down and worship me." Jesus said to him, "Away from me, Satan! For it is written: 'Worship the Lord your God, and serve him only.'"

—Matthew 4:8–10

The heart of worship knows God's character.

How did Clark Kent pull it off? How did he convincingly hide his secret identity as Superman? How did he fool everyone into thinking he was a mild-mannered reporter and not a superhuman being in tights?

No one knew his true character. They accepted Clark at face value—his coworkers and associates never thought to look past those glasses and all they represented to see the true face of Superman underneath them.

In tempting Jesus, the Devil tried to take Jesus' eyes off God and put them onto something material. Kingdoms. Splendor. But unlike Clark Kent's buddies, Jesus wasn't fooled by Satan's glasses—he knew what was up and countered Satan's character by leaning on God's character.

Jesus immediately confounded his Enemy by quoting a passage of Scripture that contradicted the Devil's statements. He called the Devil's bluff. He knocked off Satan's glasses and exposed that big "S" on his chest. Jesus knew God's character, so he wasn't fooled for a minute when promised the power and splendor of the material world.

**God's character is worth knowing.
It is worth our wholehearted devotion.
It is worth our worship.**

Prayer for the Day:

God, thanks for being so consistent in who you are. I love knowing that you're always the same, no matter what. Help me to recognize your character, Lord, so that I can worship you in spirit and in truth. The more I know your character, the more I'll recognize the Devil's counterfeits. I love you, and I want to know you more. Amen.

DAY 23: King of Endless Worth

You alone are the LORD. You made the heavens, even the highest heavens, and all their starry host, the earth and all that is on it, the seas and all that is in them. You give life to everything, and the multitudes of heaven worship you.

—NEHEMIAH 9:6

The heart of worship is in tune with songs of God's creation.

Have you ever been to the symphony? If you have, you've probably noticed that before the performance begins, all the instruments—from the flute to the bassoon, the trumpet to the tuba, the violin to the bass—play a single note in order to tune themselves to each other. And then the conductor raises his baton, and off they go.

Dipping and soaring, resting and playing, the various instruments of the symphony all have their part to play in service to the greater piece of music. On their own, they're interesting, but together, they're absorbing.

God's creation is a symphony in itself. Everything he made worships him in its own way, and looking at the world he created as a whole, we can hear strains of the great symphony he's simultaneously composing and conducting. The heart of worship hears this symphony and yearns to contribute its own voice.

But to make our contribution, we must be in tune with the greater piece of music.

We must be in tune with God's heart so that we can play our part the way he intended. It all begins with worship of the King of Endless Worth.

Prayer for the Day:

God, you are the Great Conductor, the Magnificent Composer. I pray that my heart would beat in time with your symphony, Lord, that my voice would blend with what you're doing in this world. Lord, where I'm out of tune, please help me to get back on track with your will. Thank you. Amen.

DAY 24: King of Endless Worth

Who has measured the waters in the hollow of his hand, or with the breadth of his hand marked off the heavens? Who has held the dust of the earth in a basket, or weighed the mountains on the scales and the hills in a balance? Who has understood the mind of the LORD, or instructed him as his counselor? Whom did the LORD consult to enlighten him, and who taught him the right way? Who was it that taught him knowledge or showed him the path of understanding? Surely the nations are like a drop in a bucket; they are regarded as dust on the scales; he weighs the islands as though they were fine dust.

—ISAIAH 40:12–15

The heart of worship knows its place.

Somewhere in the world right now, an ant is slowly walking toward its anthill, carrying a crumb thirty times its own weight. In the overall picture of the world, this ant is insignificant. Its singular activities will hardly have an impact on the globe. It is a drop in the bucket. It is regarded as dust on the scales.

In many ways, we are like this ant. Compared to the greatness of God, we mean nothing. He is indeed a King of Endless Worth, and we are a people headed to a worthless end.

And yet, to the ant colony, that ant is important. God did create that ant, and he gave it a specific purpose to carry out. The ant isn't a big deal to the world at large, but it is a big deal in its own world.

Again, we are like the ant. We are simultaneously unimportant to the world and *the most* important thing to God. He is the King of

Endless Worth, and, by loving us, he shares that worth with us.

We are both the dust of the earth *and* extremely valuable to God. We must remember our place and remember that we are made worthy because the King of Endless Worth has made us that way.

Let us never forget this in our worship of him; it is yet another reason to give him the glory he deserves.

Prayer for the Day:

Lord, thank you for making me worthy. Thank you for looking into my depths and giving me importance. I realize that apart from you, I genuinely have nothing. I have worth only because you are infinitely worthy. I worship you, Lord, and I pray that I will always maintain an awareness of my place. Amen.

DAY 25: No One Could Express

Blessed are you who give yourselves over to GOD, turn your backs on the world's "sure thing," ignore what the world worships; the world's a huge stockpile of GOD-wonders and GOD-thoughts. Nothing and no one comes close to you! I start talking about you, telling what I know, and quickly run out of words. Neither numbers nor words account for you.

—PSALM 40:4–5 MSG

The heart of worship is appropriately quiet.

Shh. Listen.

What do you hear? It all depends on where you are, but most likely you're hearing something you wouldn't have heard unless you purposely listened for it. Maybe it's the hum of the climate control or wind rustling the leaves of the trees or, if it's quiet enough, the beat of your own heart. You could be hearing the slight rustle of your fingers against the pages of this book or the almost imperceptible shift of your legs as you rearrange them.

It's easy to drown out all of these sounds, especially in our current culture of loudness. Worship is especially prone to being full of sound, and even the quiet times of corporate worship often involve slight background music. It seems as though we can never stop talking to God, singing to God.

But in this psalm, David readily admits that he runs out of words when trying to talk about God. Not only does he run out of them, he runs out "quickly." It doesn't take him much time to come up short for an accurate description of God's love and wonder.

So what should we do when we run out of words? Perhaps we should try listening, getting appropriately quiet before him in stillness and reverence, tuning our hearts toward God in an effort to hear—truly hear—what he desires to speak to us.

Let us learn to listen.

Prayer for the Day:

Lord God, I'm sorry I don't always take the time to listen to you. Help me to learn to love stillness and quiet. Help me to hear you when you speak quietly. I pray that you wouldn't always have to shout at me, Lord, but that I would learn to listen for your whispers. I long to hang on every word from you, God. Speak to me. Amen.

DAY 26: How Much You Deserve

Shadrach, Meshach and Abednego replied to the king, "O Nebuchadnezzar, we do not need to defend ourselves before you in this matter. If we are thrown into the blazing furnace, the God we serve is able to save us from it, and he will rescue us from your hand, O king. But even if he does not, we want you to know, O king, that we will not serve your gods or worship the image of gold you have set up."

—DANIEL 3:16–18

The heart of worship is loyal.

There they were—Shadrach, Meshach, and Abednego—faced with certain death in the fiery furnace. Reading this story, it's easy to see how confident they were in God. God was their ace in the hole—they didn't need to fear the fire, because God would rescue them, right? That was the whole reason they spoke so confidently to Nebuchadnezzar, because they *knew* they'd get through the ordeal alive.

Right?

Nope.

Check out verse 18. "Even if [God] does not [rescue us], we want you to know, O king, that we will not serve your gods or worship the image of gold you have set up."

Well, this changes things a bit, doesn't it? Now their bravado is more admirable. Shadrach, Meshach, and Abednego had no guarantee that they would survive their punishment at the hands of Nebuchadnezzar. There was no ace in the hole, no confidence that they would come out alive.

But they were still loyal to God.

God deserves that type of loyalty.

All his people should have hearts like that—hearts that are unswervingly loyal to him. Hearts that trust his ultimate will. Hearts that long to please him, no matter what the consequences. Hearts of true, loyal worship.

Prayer for the Day:

Lord Jesus, I'm so thankful that you're loyal to me. You always forgive me; you always love me, no matter what. I pray that you would instill in me a heart of loyalty. I desire to be loyal to you, but I know I won't be able to carry out that desire without your help. Help me, then, Jesus. Amen.

DAY 27: Though I'm Weak and Poor

The LORD turned to him and said, "Go in the strength you have and save Israel out of Midian's hand. Am I not sending you?" "But Lord," Gideon asked, "how can I save Israel? My clan is the weakest in Manasseh, and I am the least in my family." The LORD answered, "I will be with you, and you will strike down all the Midianites together."

—JUDGES 6:14–16

The heart of worship doesn't focus on its weakness.

Midian was bad news, crushing Israel with its mighty military force. The time had come for the Israelites to throw off the Midianite oppression, and God had chosen Gideon for the task. Israel would finally be free, and Gideon would lead the Israelites there.

Except Gideon wasn't really pleased with God's choice. God tells him what he's supposed to do, and he immediately starts arguing: "How can I save Israel? My clan is the weakest in Manasseh, and I am the least in my family." No way can I do this, God. I'm too weak and too poor.

Notice God's response to this. God didn't say, "Oh, but you're really strong, Gideon. You can do it! You're the best!" No, God simply said, "Don't sweat it. I'll be with you."

Yes, we are weak and poor, but we have God on our side. Operating through him, we become strong. It isn't through our own strength, because on our own we have no strength. But God is with us, saying, "Don't sweat your weaknesses. I'm with you."

The heart full of worship recognizes this and focuses on God's strength instead of its own weaknesses.

Prayer for the Day:

O Lord, I thank you that you choose to flex your strength through me. It isn't always easy to follow through on what you would have me to do, especially because sometimes I feel like I'm not up to the task. But nevertheless, I trust you. And if you tell me to do something, I pray that you'll give me the strength to do it. Amen.

DAY 28:
All I Have Is Yours

Your attitude should be the same as that of Christ Jesus: who, being in very nature God, did not consider equality with God something to be grasped, but made himself nothing, taking the very nature of a servant, being made in human likeness. And being found in appearance as a man, he humbled himself and became obedient to death—even death on a cross!

—PHILIPPIANS 2:5-8

The heart of worship is responsive.

"Responsive" is a word that has been adopted by the automobile industry. So many vehicles now offer "responsive" handling or "responsive" engines. What do these manufacturers mean when they use the word? They mean that their vehicles have been engineered to have no choice in the matter. If you crank the wheel, the car will turn immediately in that direction. If you gun the accelerator, you can expect the car to take off.

The car responds to whatever you tell it to do. It can do nothing *but* respond, really, if it is in working order.

But what if that car breaks down? It can no longer respond in the way it was designed. It must first be repaired before it can operate correctly.

When we were in sin, we were a broken-down vehicle. But thanks to the work that Jesus did on the cross, we've been repaired. We are now *able* to function the way we were *meant* to function. We are able to worship him completely, with abandon, without fear. We are able to see Jesus as he is and respond to him appropriately.

Jesus gave us everything he had, so we must in turn give him everything we have. It is all his, anyway, and we wouldn't have it if he hadn't repaired us. How can we respond any differently?

Prayer for the Day:

Jesus, first and foremost, thank you for saving me. Thank you for repairing me to function the way I was meant to function. I owe you so much, Jesus—my whole life. So I give you everything. It's all yours, anyway, so I give it back to you. Help me not to hang on to it. Amen.

DAY 29: All I Have Is Yours

My counsel for you is simple and straightforward: Just go ahead with what you've been given. You received Christ Jesus, the Master; now live him. You're deeply rooted in him. You're well constructed upon him. You know your way around the faith. Now do what you've been taught. School's out; quit studying the subject and start living it! And let your living spill over into thanksgiving.

—COLOSSIANS 2:6–7 MSG

The heart of worship takes action.

We've all heard the old saying "Talk is cheap." And it's true—it's very easy to say that we'll do something or that we'll act a certain way. It is much more difficult to truly change our behavior and live up to our words.

So, in the context of this song, it's an easy enough thing to sing, "All I have is yours." But what do we do when it comes to following through on that? What do we do when God asks us to quit studying that particular subject and start living what we profess?

What do we do when God directs us to give a little more money in the offering this week?

What do we do when God wants us to wake up a little earlier to pray?

What do we do when God asks us to love someone who is maybe a little less than lovable?

When we say, "All I have is yours," do we mean it? Do we really mean it, or is it just a phrase in a worship song? Is it just a lyric we sing on Sunday, or is it a lifestyle we practice throughout the week?

God wants us to mean it. Everything we have is a gift from him, anyway. He just wants us to recognize that fact and live an openhanded life.

He wants us to take action on what we say, for that is the sign of a true heart of worship.

Prayer for the Day:

Okay, God. Everything I have—it's all yours to do with as you please. I don't want to be a child about this; I don't want to throw a fit when you tell me to do something. Possessions, time, family, relationships, health—they're all yours, God. Just tell me what to do with them, and I'll obey. Amen.

DAY 30: Every Single Breath

For this is what the high and lofty One says—he who lives forever, whose name is holy: "I live in a high and holy place, but also with him who is contrite and lowly in spirit, to revive the spirit of the lowly and to revive the heart of the contrite. I will not accuse forever, nor will I always be angry, for then the spirit of man would grow faint before me—the breath of man that I have created. I was enraged by his sinful greed; I punished him, and hid my face in anger, yet he kept on in his willful ways. I have seen his ways, but I will heal him; I will guide him and restore comfort to him, creating praise on the lips of the mourners in Israel. Peace, peace, to those far and near," says the LORD. "And I will heal them."

—ISAIAH 57:15–19

The heart of worship is forgiven and healed.

We can learn a lot from the nation of Israel, God's chosen people. Reading today's passage, we can see how God really felt about his people. At this point in its history, Israel had established a consistent pattern of turning away from God. Time and time again, they would turn away, feel sorry, repent, be forgiven, and turn away again.

But speaking through the prophet Isaiah, God reminded Israel—and us—that every breath we have is one that he created. Even the breaths we drew while stumbling away from him were generous gifts from him.

And yet he still loves us enough to continue giving us breath, despite our disobedience. He looks beyond our faults and gives us the very breath we need to praise him.

The best part is that God promises us that he doesn't want our breath to grow faint. He promises to forgive us and to heal us.

And that is why we can have a heart of worship, a true heart that is intimately in love with God. Because he has forgiven and healed us.

He has kindly given us the very breath we use to bless his name. Let us lift it to him thankfully.

Prayer for the Day:

God, thank you for the breath I'm using right now to pray this prayer. I thank you for blessing me with a heart that worships you, a heart that longs to know you better. I thank you that I have air in my lungs and blood in my veins. I thank you for every single breath I take, God. I pray that I would always use them to praise you, for you are greatly to be praised. Amen.

Additional copies of this and other Honor products
are available wherever good books are sold.

Other titles in this series:

Here I Am to Worship

Blessed Be Your Name

In Christ Alone

Better Is One Day

Let Everything That Has Breath

If you have enjoyed this book, or if it has had an
impact on your life, we would like to hear from you.

Please contact us at:

Honor Books
Cook Communications Ministries, Dept. 201
4050 Lee Vance View
Colorado Springs, CO 80918

Or visit our Web site:
www.cookministries.com